7 Leadership Principles
-of-
Service and Success

CJ Rhodes

Published by
GWW Publishing
www.gwwpublishing.com

Providing Publishing Services for Christian Authors & Organizations: Hardbacks, Paperbacks, E-Books & Audiobooks.

7 Leadership Principles of Service and Success

Copyright © 2018 CJ Rhodes.

All rights reserved. Printed in the United States of America. No part of this book may be used or reproduced in any manner whatsoever without written permission except in the case of brief quotations em-bodied in critical articles or reviews.

www.cjrhodes.org

ISBN: 978-0-9991975-9-2

First Edition: March 2018

10 9 8 7 6 5 4 3 2 1

TABLE OF CONTENTS

Introduction	1
Principle 1: Prayer & Preparation	9
Principle 2: Receive & Release	19
Principle 3: Criticism & Praise	27
Principle 4: Service & Success	37
Principle 5: Low & Slow	47
Principle 6: Shade & Shine	55
Principle 7: Pain & Pleasure	63
About the Author	71

Introduction

When Martin Luther King, Jr. became pastor of Dexter Avenue Baptist Church in 1954, he had no intentions of leading a movement. The twenty-five-year-old preacher was finishing up his doctoral studies at Boston University and was a relatively newlywed husband, having married, his bride, Coretta less than a year before answering the call to serve Montgomery's prestigious black congregation. It was his first pastorate and his ambitious goals for revitalizing the church took precedent over everything else. But as soon as he was settling in, Mrs. Rosa Parks amplified a movement with her refusal to give up her seat on a city bus. Black leaders soon gathered and determined that a bus boycott was the best action to take. Though Pastor King was selected to serve as the leader of the Montgomery Improvement Association, King biographer Clayborn Carson calls him a reluctant civil rights leader, made one by the courage of Mrs. Parks and, to some degree, the cowardice of several of Montgomery's older ministers. The trajectory of Dr. King's life radically changed in 1955 and the thirteen years of public activism that carried him from Montgomery to Memphis were full of leadership moments far beyond the shadow of a small-town pulpit.

Fifty years after his assassination his dream, his eloquence, and his prophetic daring still resonate with people from around the world and across generations. A national holiday exists in his honor, streets in cities around the country are named after him, and his brilliant reflections on faith and justice still stir us to action. Dr. King's leadership causes many to ask, "Where is our generation's Dr. King?" What made this fourth-generation preacher and reluctant civil rights leader so iconic? What pushed him from national obscurity to global notoriety? The answer to these questions may shock you.

I assume you are reading this book because you are a leader or aspiring to be a better one. Like me, you may admire leaders like Dr. King and hope to do a fraction of what they did. Dr. King was indeed a visionary, intelligent, and courageous. All good qualities any solid leader should have. But beyond these qualities is something that qualified him for global impact. Beyond his pedigree, degrees, accolades, and the like is the one key ingredient every leader who wants to be used mightily by God must have. Are you ready for it?

Dr. King had humility. God exalted Dr. King because he was humble.

This book is about leadership. Better yet, it's about humility expressed through service to others. What made Dr. King great is the same means for greatness any of us have access to. Exactly two months before his assassination in 1968, Dr. King preached a message titled "The Drum Major Instinct." In it he encouraged his listeners to identify greatness in a way that then and now is countercultural. Many would-be leaders have this drum major instinct. We want to be out front, on the stage, behind the mic, and on top of the world. King submitted that there is nothing wrong with this instinct if it isn't distorted, but we should seek to be the number one servant. He preached:

> *And this morning, the thing that I like about it: by giving that definition of greatness, it means that everybody can be great, because everybody can serve. You don't have to have a college degree to serve. You don't have to make your subject and your verb agree to serve. You don't have to know about Plato and Aristotle to serve. You don't have to know Einstein's theory of relativity to serve. You don't have to know the second theory of thermodynamics in physics to serve. You only need a heart full of grace, a soul generated by love. And you*

can be that servant.[1]

"The greatest among you shall be your servant," said Jesus to His disciples. (Matthew 23:11) Greatness is measured not by how high you sit, but by how well you serve! Dr. King and countless other heroes and sheroes we look up to were great because they lived their lives in service to others and the common good. They were successful because they served.

For twenty years God has blessed me with various leadership roles. In high school, I was the president of my tenth-grade class and went on to single-handedly rewrite our student government constitution the following year. I was appointed to our school board as a student representative where I advocated for our needs and concerns. Subsequently, in college, I served in various student government positions, eventually co-founding the department of minority affairs and serving

---

[1] http://kingencyclopedia.stanford.edu/encyclopedia/documentsentry/doc_the_drum_major_instinct/

on the Chancellor's Committee for Respect and Sensitivity. God blessed me with other leadership opportunities in divinity school, and when I was led back to my home state after receiving my masters of divinity, I served a statewide ministry, became the youngest pastor of Jackson's oldest black church, and a chaplain at Alcorn State University.

      I do not share this resume in order to boast in myself but to brag on God. You see, in most of these endeavors I was provided space to lead in very successful ways because I was willing to serve. I found favor with God and people around me, the latter often seeing more in me than I could see in myself. Seldom have I asked for a position. Literally, people have reached out to me, inviting me to opportunities beyond my wildest imagination. I haven't had to politic or prostitute myself. God has opened the doors and I simply walk through them. And as a good Southerner, I have always told God and those He used to hold the door open for me, "Thank you!"

If you get nothing else from this book, I offer this to you: *God gives his favor to those He trusts will give Him His glory!* When you're humble, you are willing to serve. As a result, God breathes on your service and gives it good success. God can mightily use you when know it's really not about you.

In the succeeding chapters I want to give you seven principles that flow from this conviction about the relationship between humility and leadership, between service and success. The seven principles are as follows:

1. Prayer and Preparation: Pray like it all depends on God. Prepare like it all depends on you.
2. Receive and Release: You must know yourself intimately before your show yourself publicly.
3. Criticism and Praise: Don't let criticism go to your heart and praise go to your head.

4. Service and Success: Measure your greatness by how well you serve, not by how successful you are.
5. Low and Slow: Speed determines your arrival time, but significance determines your staying time.
6. Shade and Shine: Don't dim the light of your leadership by casting shade on others.
7. Pain and Pleasure: Every leader has a thorn. Know yours.

These seven principles have blessed me for nearly two decades and I hope they will bless you too.

PRINCIPLE 1

Prayer and Preparation

Pray like it all depends on God. Prepare like it all depends on you.

Leaders are decision makers. Yes, leaders possess influence, clear vision, and a sense of direction. But what makes a leader a leader is that she or he is *leading* people and organizations somewhere. In order to move a group from A to B, you must make decisions. Decision making is easier said than done. As a pastor and HBCU chaplain, my respect for leaders from all spheres of life has grown significantly. One thing I can't stand is for folks to coach from the stands. It's always easier to say what should be done when you're not in the game.

Actual leaders are in the game, making the plays and feeling the bumps and bruises of a contact sport. As I have interviewed and counseled ministers, elected officials and business people, the theme is the same: leaders face tough decisions often connected to the well-being of their followers, employees, members, or even family members. Decision making isn't for the faint of heart and requires wisdom far beyond our capacities.

One leader I know had a major crisis. At the helm of a large institution, he faced major budget cuts and layoffs. He surveyed all the available data and came away with a painful reality: tough choices and unpopular decisions had to be made in order to ensure the institution's longevity. He came to me for advice, trusting that there is safety in a multitude of counsel. (Proverbs 11:14) I honestly didn't know what advice to give him, though, seeing that his budget was ten times the one I manage. What I did know is that he was in a precarious situation and needed to proceed cautiously, wisely.

"Have you prayed about it?" I asked, not knowing what else to say. My friend looked at me quizzically, certainly taken aback. After hesitating a few seconds, he replied, "No. That's why I'm talking to you."

Beside my better judgement, I told my friend I really had nothing more to say to him, but that maybe God had much more to say if only he took his issue to the Lord in prayer. My friend is smart and had planned to occupy his present position since he was a teenager. He had the goods but needed something more in this moment. I invited him to pray with me then and there. If we touched and agreed, I thought, surely the Lord would hear and answer.

Thankfully, God did answer. And, oh, how God answered. Before our time in prayer, my friend assumed he only had two options. Option one was to do nothing and keep doing business as usual until things got worse. The second option was to make big cuts, which would mean several people would lose their jobs, potentially causing protests against his leadership. He knew the first option was a no go; his fears about "what's next" kept him from committing to the second option.

After our prayer, however, he discovered that there was, in fact, a third option. Before then, he didn't see that there was room to make adjustments without laying off so many employees. A new piece of information was given to him before the decision deadline and it changed the game. God made a way out of no way. It turned out that my friend's decision made the institution stronger and even made him more popular.

Prayer works. Or better, prayer taps into God's supply. Let me be clear: I am not advocating for prayer apart from preparation. Too many people are not where they want to be not because they aren't praying, but because they aren't preparing from what they want from God. So, when opportunity arrives they aren't ready to receive. Nevertheless, you can be a well prepared leader who still makes wrong decisions. How many people do you know who look like they have it all together but for some reason they never seem to win at life and leadership? They're missing something, no, someone, from their success equation.

If you want to be successful in leadership, I encourage you to take every advantage out there to prepare yourself. Study hard, network, work on your weaknesses and play to your strengths. Be the best you you can be. When you have accumulated all of your degrees, certifications, connections, and the like, know that there will be tough decisions you will need to make that no amount of preparation will have equipped you for. I experienced this when I started pastoring. I was trained in theology at one of the world's top universities where I studied with leading scholars. Before that I served other pastors in churches of varying sizes and visions. Soon after being called to pastor, I learned how much I didn't know. I needed divine wisdom in order to handle some tough decisions and I could only get that wisdom from God alone.

In fact, pastoring taught me something. I had spent my earlier years coaching from the bleachers. Young and ambitious, I often thought I knew better than the pastors I served. How wrong I was! I knew very little about how to manage diverse people who have divergent wants and needs. Shepherding God's sheep felt more like herding cats and I couldn't understand why. I thought I was saying and doing all the right things. God had to show me that in order to move the church forward in healthy ways I needed to rely more on Him than on my preparation. Likewise, many other times my yes to God's best in my leadership journey happened after prayer. When friends ask me why I decided on this or that, I say I prayed about it first. Servant leaders are aware enough of themselves to know that they don't have all the answers. God does. God is omniscient, which is a fancy way of saying God knows everything. When we edge God out (EGO), we deny ourselves of better and wiser solutions to our nagging problems. Prayer is the humble acknowledgement that we are limited but God is infinite. We can access divine abundance by simply engaging in conversation with our Creator.

Before you think that prayer is motivated by a certain kind of weakness, let me remind you that Jesus prayed before making major decisions. Here was the Word made flesh, for whom and by whom all things were made, going away to pray before big moments in His earthly ministry. In a compelling passage found in Luke 6:12-13, we are told, "In these days he went out to the mountain to pray, and all night he continued in prayer to God. And when day came, he called his disciples and chose from them twelve, whom he named apostles:" Do you see that? Before Jesus chose His disciples, His leadership team, those who would continue His mission in His name after His death, burial and resurrection, He prayed *all night.*

One of the areas where I have failed a few times in leadership is choosing team members without praying. Let's just say things never work out for me when I try to lead with someone not ordained to walk with me. Often out of desperation, I've too quickly called upon someone to lead with me, only to regret the decision soon thereafter. These persons haven't been wicked; it's just that we didn't have the right rhythm and found ourselves tripping over each other while trying to walk together. Jesus pulled an all-nighter before calling the Twelve. Yes, one turned out to be a devil, and the rest were disappointing in many instances, but they (excluding Judas) would go on to turn the world upside down! They were chosen *after* prayer.

The other big prayer moment was right before Jesus' betrayal and crucifixion. There He was in the Garden of Gethsemane, awaiting His suffering, praying that the bitter cup would pass from Him. Here we see our Lord as vulnerable before His Father, honest about the tension between His will and His Father's will. He submitted to His destiny after wrestling in prayer. Friend, there are some things in your leadership that won't get resolved until you learn how to wrestle with it in prayer.

You have some decisions to make. Many of them are tough, and surely none of them are really easy. Leaders handle big issues, not small ones. No matter how intelligent, educated, and networked we may be, there are some things we won't press through, achieve, and grow from until we take things to the Lord in prayer. One of the best ways to success is to pray your way to it.

Trust in the Lord with all thine heart; and lean not unto thine own understanding. In all thy ways acknowledge him, and he shall direct thy paths.

Proverbs 3:5-6

PRINCIPLE

Receive and Release

You must know yourself intimately before your show yourself publicly.

In chapter one I shared how important prayer is in making life-changing decisions. Your leadership is the better when you serve with God's best in view and you access that vision and receive those blessings through prayer. Cultivating spiritual practices like prayer is a sure way to be successful according to God's design.

Turning to our second principle, I may have made a wrong assumption and I want to address it in this chapter. My possibly wrong assumption is that you want to be successful. Doesn't everyone? Well, not really. There are many people who are afraid of success. They self-sabotage every good thing God gives them. Healthy relationships, career advancements, and new opportunities are forfeited when we've been mastered by mediocrity so long that we can't even recognize success when it shows up.

I know this because throughout my life I've been afraid of success. Having grown up in Hazlehurst, Mississippi, a small railroad town about forty-five miles south of Jackson, I thought Nathanael was talking about my hometown when he asked, "Can anything good come out of Nazareth?" (John 1:46) There was not much going for Hazlehurst in the 1980's and '90's when I was growing up and I couldn't wait to move away after high school to some cosmopolitan city on the East Coast.

We were also poor in the early years of my childhood and I blamed myself when my parents divorced when I was six. Given our state's racial history, I warred between loving my blackness and mourning my broad nostrils and thick lips. If that wasn't enough, I had social anxiety that showed up in stammering speech whenever I got nervous. My public school wasn't the best, so even when universities around the country sent letters to me and offered me scholarships during high school, I just knew I wasn't smart enough to survive a Duke or Morehouse. Whenever I got close to "doing it big", I found some reason to shut the door on that opportunity. I was the assassin of my success.

It took me getting into my 20s to actually feel that I was somebody. By that time, I had already accomplished a lot as a leader. I was celebrated by my peers and professors alike while leading at the University of Mississippi. For some reason, I couldn't shake this feeling of inadequacy. I can't count the numbers of times I was rejected by girls I had crushes on, or how many times something reminded me that due to my financial circumstances growing up I didn't experience special things around the world. These experiences compounded to make me doubt my abilities and the possibility of ascending to heights unknown. I had to finally receive that God not only cared for me greatly, but also that God called me to greatness! This receiving happened first in my spirit before it reached my mind. I had to believe it before I could think it. I "faithed" my way into acceptance.

Now, as I said in the introduction, each of us can be great because each of us can serve (Dr. King said it, but you get the point). Let me add that each of us can serve when we say yes to what God wants us to do. Saying yes, though, isn't easy. Flip through the pages of the Bible and you are confronted with men and women called to do great things for God and who protested. Have you noticed that when God called, many of them threw up an excuse, an insecurity? Moses had a stuttering problem. Gideon was from a small tribe. Jeremiah was too young. In almost every instance the Lord said to them something like this: Fear not! I got you!

It's often hard for those of us with deep insecurities to see ourselves as God and others see us. Fear not! God's got you! What you must embrace is the notion that I must receive everything God is doing in me and through me. In turn, you have to release the self-images that hold you back from giving the kingdom and the world the best service you have to give them.

One of my favorite stories in the Bible is about when Mary received the angelic visitation announcing that she would give birth to the Messiah. In Luke 1:28-29 we read, "And he came to her and said, "Greetings, O favored one, the Lord is with you!" But she was greatly troubled at the saying, and tried to discern what sort of greeting this might be."

Mary, a poor girl from the ghettos of Galilee heard a divine message. *She* was blessed and highly favored and the Lord was with her. The text says she was *greatly* troubled by the word. This is the CJV (CJ Version): Maybe she was troubled because she couldn't see herself as blessed and highly favored. Here she was, a young peasant from an obscure place. How could she be favored? The answer, in part, is that her circumstances qualified her to be blessed. God's favor is attracted to the least, the lost, the looked over, and the left behind. God exalts the humble and chooses foolish things to make the wise of the world scratch their heads.

Listen to me: God wants to do mighty things through your leadership. Maybe you came from a rough part of town. Maybe you were a teen parent. Maybe you don't have the best grammar or aren't well connected. So what? With God, all things are possible. Your demography isn't your destiny. Your delays aren't your denials. Receive that God wants to use you for His glory and release all of the low self-esteem, self-sabotage, and self-doubt that keeps you from releasing the gifts and anointing God has stored up in you. There's treasure in your earthen vessel. Open yourself up to God so that God can release your treasures for the common good.

I'm telling you something I had to tell myself numerous times. I've had to speak it until I could see it. Thankfully, I've had the blessing of others speaking into my life. Earlier I talked about my speech problem. So many people don't believe it because I speak for a living now! I suppressed my fear of public speaking because my high school oral communication teacher believed in me. One day while sitting together at the lunch table, she told me that I was to deliver one of Dr. Martin Luther King Jr.'s speeches at the upcoming Black History Month program. I protested, "No ma'am. I don't want to do it." "I'm not asking you to do it. I'm telling you that you are going to do it," she replied. She then slid an audio cassette to me (this was before CD's and YouTube). It had several of Dr. King's speeches. "Listen to this and be ready to deliver the speech." I was terrified!

For the next several days I listened and rehearsed. When the day of the program came, I was absolutely nervous, but I got through the speech. Greeted by a standing ovation at it's conclusion of the speech, I knew that something miraculous happened. Little did I know at that time that I would travel the region delivering MLK speeches at churches and youth events. Less did I know that a year later God would call me into the ministry. It was if God used my teacher to prepare me for the public ministry to which God was calling me. Because I received, I am now able to release.

Don't be afraid. You're favored!

God chose what is low and despised in the world, even things that are not, to bring to nothing things that are,

1 Corinthians 1:28

PRINCIPLE

Criticism and Praise

Don't let criticism go to your heart and praise go to your head.

There are two things that can wreck your leadership, especially if you have ever dealt with low self-esteem and insecurities: criticism and praise. Criticism and praise have a way of eating away at your soul in different, yet powerful ways. Every leader has encountered and will encounter these two realities, and they often walk together, sometimes in the same person. I have discovered that you will have critics no matter how strong and visionary your leadership is. I've also learned that those who praise you today may hate on you tomorrow. It comes with the territory.

As I shared in the last chapter, I have a history with low self-esteem and rejection. That has historically made me especially prone to seek out affirmation and to wallow in pity when criticized. Truth is, I've often wanted everyone to like me. I guess it's because I've not been accepted by so many people in younger years. The danger in this mindset is that we can seek out attention and affirmation to a degree that we erode proper boundaries. To that end, we lose ourselves in the company of other people's opinions. As I've often said, be careful of applause for the same hands that clap for you now may crush you later.

Leaders must seek the welfare of the

led. You can't do that if you are always trying to get the led to like you. It's been said that you should desire respect over being well-liked. I don't think those two are mutually exclusive, but when you expend too much energy to get people to like you, you sacrifice the will to serve them in ways they may not at first like, but which are for their good in the long run.

So, watch the desire to be liked. There was a moment in my leadership journey when I was saying yes to everyone's requests. I showed up to myriad events, advocated various causes, and attached my influence to people I barely knew. I believed in these ventures to a degree, but I wasn't being true to what Howard Thurman advised when he said, "Don't ask what the world needs. Ask what makes you come alive." I found myself sometimes doing what was necessary but not life giving. Saying no was poisonous, I thought, because people expect so much from their leaders. What I discovered as I neared burnout is that while I was saying yes to everyone, I was slowly saying no to my best self. Losing myself in other's demands, I had to reposition and center myself. Thankfully, I'm an introvert so I know how to go within. Through prayer and meditation, I learned that there is a gift in saying no and goodbye. It meant, however, being okay with not being liked.

It seems nowadays our culture is producing leaders who are overly sensitive and overly responsive to criticism. Social media has made it easier to attack and to counter-attack. There was a season in which I got tired of seeing people subtweeting about their haters. A friend of mine said that too many leaders need to put down their smartphones and sit on a therapist's couch. Ouch! My friend is right. Giving too much attention to critics is a sign that there is something unresolved in us. That sensitivity may result from childhood or adulthood trauma, or some moment in which our mind is stuck. Until we free ourselves from that, we may always die a thousand deaths at the tip of someone's tongue.

To be sure, not all criticism is bad. Sometimes it's constructive. Constructive criticism is meant to build you up, not to tear you down. Humble leaders are always open to friendly amendments, diverse perspectives, and challenging words. A true friend will tell you when you're wrong. A true leader will accept when she or he is wrong and correct course.

However, there's a difference between constructive and destructive criticism. The latter is motivated by a drive to tear down anyone that is more successful than they are. Success attracts haters. Winning attracts whiners. You can't let it go to your heart. Dr. King said that if he responded to every criticism, he wouldn't have time for constructive work. You have too much to do to sit around worried about who doesn't like you or what you're offering through your leadership.

Don't let it go to your heart. One of my struggles was that one hundred people can tell me I did a great job, but that one person that criticized me would cause me to grieve for at least three days. I had to get to the point, though, when I asked, "Why does that person have that much power over my mood?" Oftentimes, we allow the words of our critics to occupy emotional space rent-free and blame them for being there. Today, evict negative words, people, and experiences from your heart and from this day forward guard your heart from those who seek to tear you down. It's not worth the stress and heartache.

Likewise, be careful to not become intoxicated with praise. Social media is also good for maximizing our craving for attention. Our lust for likes causes us to monitor our apps constantly to see who liked our comment or photo. We end up measuring how popular or successful we are by how many "friends" shared our video. One of the dangers is that this type of superficial affirmation can go to our head. So many of us are puffed up because we believe our own press.

There's a story from the Desert Fathers that really drives this third principle home. I share it below:

A brother once came to the abbot Macarius and said to him, "Master, speak some word of exhortation to me, that, obeying it, I may be saved." St. Macarius answered him, "Go to the tombs and attack the dead with insults." The brother wondered at the word. Nevertheless, he went, as he was bidden, and cast stones at the tombs, railing upon the dead. Then returning, he told what he had done. Macarius asked him, "Did the dead notice what you did?" And he replied, "They did not notice me."

"Go, then, again," said Macarius, "and this time praise them." The brother, wondering yet more, went and praised the dead, calling them just men, apostles, saints. Returning, he told what he had done, saying, "I have praised the

dead."

Macarius asked him, "Did they reply to you?" And he said, "They did not reply to me." Then said Macarius, "You know what insults you have heaped on them and with what praises you have flattered them, and yet they never spoke to you. If you desire salvation, you must be like these dead. You must think nothing of the wrongs men do to you, nor of the praises they offer you. Be like the dead. Thus, you may be saved."

What Macarius taught this young brother in the Egyptian desert is what we must constantly learn today. When you die to the opinion of others, you can live fully to what God ordains you to be. You come alive to your best leadership potential the moment you pick up your proverbial cross and follow Jesus into the realm of infinite possibilities, for his praise and glory alone.

Faithful are the wounds of a friend; but the kisses of an enemy are deceitful.

Proverbs 27:6

Giving too much attention to critics is a sign that there is something unresolved in us.

PRINCIPLE 4

Service and Success

Measure your greatness by how well you serve, not by how successful you are.

Beneath the shade of giant trees rests the beautiful campus of Alcorn State University. Alumni will tell you that the grass is a little greener, the air is a little cleaner, and the water is a little sweeter there. It's truly a special place, and some have gone so far as to call it a slice of heaven.

One of the things that makes Alcorn special is her people. The friendly, downhome feeling you get welcomes you like a bear hug embrace. Alcorn is synonymous with Southern hospitality. Among her friendly people are support staff members who keep the campus going. The prestigious buildings that crown rolling hills are cleaned and the emerald green grass is manicured every day by faithful custodians.

Clerical staff answer phone calls, return emails, print documents, shoot off faxes, and greet students. Food services team members prepare and serve varieties of breakfast, lunch and dinner delights. In many important ways, the staff personnel are the backbone of the university. Without them, trash would spill out into the street, the grass would be as tall as the students, and the buildings would look like haunted houses filled with cobwebs and debris.

I appreciate the work that they do and which often goes unnoticed because it's so ordinary. In a real sense, they model for us what servant leadership is all about. They are necessary but not always in the foreground. We may not always see them, but we would certainly miss them if they weren't around. I encourage every leader to take that lesson to heart. Contrary to popular opinion, leadership isn't about being seen. In fact, most of what a leader does isn't visible to the masses. It's easy to get caught up in speeches, awards, and press coverage. However, the hours of preparation, and the several moments you bless someone when the cameras aren't around is leadership at its best.

According to Jesus, the greatest leader in human history, leadership is done with service, plain and simple. When the Creator of the universe became one of us, He came to serve and not to be served. (Matthew 20:28) He took on the role of a servant (Philippians 2) and commanded His followers to likewise serve others. On the night that He was betrayed, the Gospel of John tells us Jesus was washing His disciples' feet after supper. (John 13:12-17) Even the Lord of glory was willing to get His hands dirty. Serving others with dignity is at the center and circumference of excellent leadership for those who emulate the Suffering Servant. Too many leaders want the title but haven't picked up the towel of service. Those leaders would learn a lot from custodians, clerical staff, cafeteria workers, and Jesus.

To be clear, leadership begins with a towel, not a title. In fact, you can lead without a title, but you can't serve without a proverbial towel. Some of the nation's greatest leaders will tell you that they learned to lead by following someone else and by serving others. There are CEOs who started out as mail boys, politicians who began managing campaigns, pastors who served from the second chariot decades before sitting in the middle chair.

I was blessed to be called to pastor Mt. Helm Baptist Church in 2010, becoming the youngest pastor in the congregation's nearly two-hundred-year history. What many who celebrated that humbling accomplishment didn't know is that I was called into ministry in 2000, nearly a decade before I became a solo pastor. In those nearly ten years, I served other pastors, learned from them, and showed up to serve in whatever way they needed. Most weeks I didn't preach a sermon or teach Bible study. Sometimes I did what seemed to be menial tasks.

My pastors weren't always strategic in how they mentored me. We didn't meet once a week over coffee. I didn't take surveys and I wasn't sent to leadership development conferences. Many times, I listened to their wisdom on drives to their preaching engagements; that's the way they transferred their knowledge to me. I watched, waited, and worshipped my way to the middle chair.

Admittedly, I didn't always serve well. Youthful ambition sometimes got the best of me. That's why I am patient with young leaders who get in their own way by trying to by-pass service. But God has favored me, I believe, because more often than not I put service before self. Now that I lead in various settings, I'm looking to elevate those who have a servant's heart.

DT, one of my spiritual sons, fit that profile. We connected when I arrived at Alcorn to serve as chaplain and we quickly developed a bond. Sundays I preached in our chapel and DT was right there. I unlocked the doors at least thirty minutes before service started, and DT would be walking up the chapel steps minutes later. He showed up every Sunday, whether he was on program or not.

If I asked him to pray or to read a scripture, he simply replied, "Yes sir." He prayed for me as I ministered to his fellow students. Eventually, I gave DT a few opportunities to preach, but like my pastor mentors, I seldom had opportunity not to preach. That is, until responsibilities at the church made it difficult to be at the chapel every Sunday. When the transition came, I knew exactly what I would do. I named DT as my successor and he preached the majority of Sundays I wasn't there. He served his way to success. Never did he beg for it. God simply blessed him with it because he was found faithful in his service in "small" matters.

Friends, if God can't trust you with the small matters of leadership, why should God trust you with bigger opportunities and responsibilities. God and others are looking at you, watching you, to see if you are consistent and humble in what you do in service. The door of success is unlocked with the key of service. Find a place to serve in and watch God exalt you. Keep serving faithfully where you are planted by God and watch the favor of the Lord work in and for you. Hustling alone could never grant you these types of blessings.

As I close this chapter, I want to leave you with something that may remind you of what it means to serve. Consider these the five marks of service:

Show up. Many times, we miss God's move because we're not in the action, among the people, with a towel in our hand. Show up and ultimately, you'll see God show out on your behalf.

Excel. Have an excellent spirit as you serve. Treat the group of five with the same respect as you would the audience of five thousand. As Dr. King preached, "Sweep streets so well that all the host of heaven and earth will have to pause and say, "Here lived a great street sweeper who swept his job well!""

Rejoice for others. There's nothing like showing up for others and rejoicing with them as they are winning. Nothing stops our divine flow like jealousy. Here's the thing: when your team is winning, so are you. So celebrate the success of others even as you serve.

Value the experience. So many of us have had the experience of rushing to where we wanted to be, so much so that we didn't actually value the lessons God was teaching us in the moment. As I look back to previous service contexts, I see how much they influenced how I lead today. Value and appreciate where you are now; it will bless you for years to come.

Expect the best. If you are serving with the right motivation and with sincere intentions, God will inevitably reward your best service. See yourself in the future and praise God in advance for what you will do in His power. When you're faithful over a few things, God will raise you up!

Serve your way into success!

His lord said unto him, Well done, good and faithful servant; thou hast been faithful over a few things, I will make thee ruler over many things: enter thou into the joy of thy lord.

Matthew 25:23

Keep serving faithfully where you are planted and watch the favor of the Lord work in and for you. Hustling alone could never grant you these type of blessings.

PRINCIPLE 5

Low and Slow

Low and Slow: Speed determines your arrival time, but significance determines your staying time.

I still remember the calmness in Mark's, my older brother, baritone voice as helped me through my speech issues. From stuttering to rushing through entire sentences, the younger me wasn't to be confused with the compelling communicator I later longed to be. My problem was that I got anxious around crowds and expressing my thoughts to strangers was terrifying. Much later in life I found out that this is normal behavior for introverts, a term and identity marker I was belatedly introduced to in divinity school. Mark, however, really coached me through the worst of it and by the time God called me into ministry, I was well on my way to using my voice to influence others. Mark taught me how to slow down.

Take your time. This imperative statement doesn't only apply to making our verbal communication comprehensible. If we want staying power in leadership, we have to know how to pace ourselves. This may seem odd to your sensibilities. We live in a time of constant and rapid change. As soon as you get use to one technology or app, there's another one being marketed to the "cool kids." We are altogether impatient in ways that people weren't a generation ago.

If you want classic leadership as opposed to "one hit" leadership, you need to embrace that four letter word: W-A-I-T. Classics endure. I can still listen to James Brown or Luther Vandross and they sound as fresh as the day their songs were released. One hit wonders, however, soon wither like the green herb. There are many people who are hustling for the number one spot, only to arrive there without any staying power. If you want to be truly successful, you have to be okay with waiting, maturing, and becoming seasoned.

Joseph dreamed a dream. He was 17-years-old when God gave it to him but it took 13 years before that dream became a reality. Thirteen years! David was anointed for kingship three times (1 Samuel 16:13; 2 Samuel 2:4; 5:3) and waited seven years before he ruled Israel. So, for seven years, David had the oil but had to wait on the office! Many of us believe that when God gives us a dream, God intends to bring it to pass immediately. One lesson we learn from

Joseph's life is that deferred dreams don't equate to denied destinies. Even though the fruition of the dream may tarry, God is not slack concerning divine promises. Wait, I say, on the Lord.

I encourage you not to give up "in the meantime," that space between your divinely sanctioned dream and God's appointed time for its manifestation. The road may be riddled with rejection. Your destination may possess several detours and even distractions, but wait on it. It shall come to pass in due season.

That word had to settle into my spirit not too long ago. Like you, I'm bombarded with stories of successful leaders who periodically make me ask myself, "What am I doing with my life?" There's the pastor who took a dying church and grew the membership from fifty to five hundred in five months. There's the CEO who turned a struggling franchise into a Fortune 500 business. There's that single mom of three who quit her two jobs, invested her pension into a business idea, and is now a self-made millionaire. If I weren't saved, I'd hate all these people. But I don't hate them; they inspire me. Instead of feeling regretful about where I'm not, I remain thankful for where I am.

Since my teens I've been leading in some capacity and God has been grooming me. I know the fast track to leadership success is very attractive. I submit to you that we often only know part of the success stories we hear. On a few occasions, I've heard Bishop TD Jakes talk about how he started and how long it took him to be the international phenomenon he is today. Most successful people aren't overnight successes. Good and godly success comes with much prayer, preparation, and opportunity. And time.

I'm a foodie. My mother and grandmother instructed me in culinary arts from age twelve onward. As they prepared Sunday dinners, I stood next to them, watching each step unfold. Mom cooked us breakfast and dinner every weekday, even though we could eat breakfast and lunch at school. Then, too, I observed her dexterity. Both of these wonderful women took ordinary ingredients and performed miracles on shoestring budgets.

I dare not say I'm the best chef in town, but I've certainly learned a thing or two about cooking. What I am most thankful for is learning how to cook home cooked meals the old fashioned way. Due to the demands on my time, I don't always get to cook at home, but when I do I don't like to be rushed. The best meals require patience.

Think about eating greens at many restaurants. As good as other menu items might be, I've discovered that greens are often not as delicious when compared to Grandma's greens. Why? It takes about three or four hours to really get all of the flavors cooked into the greens. In many restaurants, the chefs are rushing to get the food out to the customers and the greens don't have time to simmer.

Some leaders are like rushed greens. There's some flavor there, but not enough to have the WOW factor. When you are slow cooked, you leave a lasting impact, not a watered-down impression. Be a slow cooked leader. It's the humble way and the lasting way.

I returned, and saw under the sun, that the race is not to the swift, nor the battle to the strong, neither yet bread to the wise, nor yet riches to men of understanding, nor yet favour to men of skill; but time and chance happeneth to them all.

Ecclesiastes 9:11

If you want to be truly successful, you have to be okay with waiting, maturing, and becoming seasoned.

PRINCIPLE 6

Shade and Shine

Don't dim the light of your leadership by casting shade on others.

If you don't want to be talked about, don't do anything of significance. Action, of any kind, attracts response, and it isn't always pleasant. In fact, most leaders who live under the spotlight of service must deal with the heat of opposition and criticism. We talked about how to handle that in chapter three. It's easy for us to identify and take offense in what others say about us, especially when it's not true. One thing leaders must guard themselves from is doing the same thing to others, particularly those who are leading in similar lanes.

We in the African American community often hear about the "crabs in the barrel" mentality. This mentality is said to produce intense competition between blacks, rather than stimulate cooperation among blacks. It's been rightly noted that if this mentality is true, it's because crabs in a barrel are not in their natural habitat. Crabs belong in oceans and on beaches, not in man-made structures that limit their mobility.

Each crab, knowing that the box isn't its home, climbs over other crabs trying to get home. As this applies to competition in the black community, many leaders are trying to achieve success by any means necessary. They are climbing out of poverty, scarcity, and limited opportunities in order to "arrive." You really can't blame the crab for trying to get out of the barrel. The problem with this notion, of course, is that competing to get out, rather than cooperating, is a sure way for most of us to stay at the bottom. You can never get too high by making everyone else look small.

We sometimes tell others to stay in their lane, to wait their turn, and to know their place, because we are intimidated by their potential. If they are better than us in any way, we think they will surely displace us. Given our historic struggle in the country, many of us are happy with being the first and only something. Too many of us aren't reaching back and reaching down as we are climbing up because we are afraid that the ones we pull up will eventually pull us down.

Upon speaking with an older leader, he told me that he fought too hard to be where he is to just give his influence and affluence away to someone he can't trust with his legacy. "They'll have to claw it from my cold, dead hands," he said sternly, making sure I understood he would die fighting for his continued relevance.

The kind of leadership I'm after and offering to you is one that trusts in God's abundance. In Matthew 6:33, our Lord says, "But seek first the kingdom of God and his righteousness, and all these things will be added to you." What are these things? Our basic needs are met when we trust in our good Father, who is rich in mercy. Notice, Jesus isn't speaking about things that bling, but these things: food, clothing, shelter.

Yes, we may gain great riches, but leadership isn't about fame and fortune, it's about significance and service. When we seek the kingdom of heaven and its righteousness and justice, God will take care of the rest. This admonition follows the Lord's model prayer (vv 7-13), in which Jesus instructs us to trust in our Father's desire to give us daily bread and deliverance from the evil one.

Insecure leaders are those who have placed their trust in everything but God. So, they are anxious about keeping their position, platform, and popularity. They tear down others, all the while dimming their light by throwing shade on others. You know I'm telling the truth. We are intoxicated with gossip. The fad nowadays is "spilling tea." In many instances, the motivation behind this is a Machiavellian one.

The intention is to discredit others so that by doing so the "spiller" can come out looking like the better, more trustworthy leader. You can get a lot of fans by throwing shade. But if you really want people to follow you, you have to have enough integrity to see yourself as just one part of a larger puzzle. In other words, none of us has it altogether. We all have blind spots and weaknesses, and there is room enough on the kingdom's stage for all of us to shine.

Paul addresses a similar issue in 1 Corinthians. The saints in the Corinthian church are divided. They are making distinctions based on status and spirituality. Using a metaphor from Human A & P, Paul writes in chapter 12:14-20

14 For the body does not consist of one member but of many. 15 If the foot should say, "Because I am not a hand, I do not belong to the body," that would not make it any less a part of the body. 16 And if the ear should say, "Because I am not an eye, I do not belong to the body," that would not make it any less a part of the body. 17 If the whole body were an eye, where would be the sense of hearing? If the whole body were an ear, where would be the sense of smell? 18 But as it is, God arranged the members in the body, each one of them, as he chose. 19 If all were a single member, where would the body be? 20 As it is, there are many parts, yet one body.

Many members, but one body. Many gifts, but one God and Giver of the gifts. When you know that all of us matter before God, it's easier to resist the temptation to insecurely rest in a superiority complex. Each part of the body, of the community, of the church, of the government, has a particular and purposeful role to play. We are all important. Servant leaders don't dim their light by casting shade on others. They see the gifts in others and seek to find places where those gifts can flourish to the glory of God.

As a leader, I've had people try to tear me down, to discredit me. I'm been talked about sure as you're born. But I refuse to use my influence or platform to reciprocate the hate. Rather, I'm plotting ways for all of us crabs to get out of the bucket. I'd rather tear down the bucket than to tear down a fellow crab. In fact, the more we tear at each other, the longer the structures and systems that hold us back will stay in place. Servant leaders who see the big picture aren't satisfied with simply being "big."

Let nothing be done through strife or vainglory; but in lowliness of mind let each esteem other better than themselves. Look not every man on his own things, but every man also on the things of others.

Philippians 2:3-4

You can get a lot of fans by throwing shade. But if you really want people to follow you, you have to have enough integrity to see yourself as just one part of a larger puzzle.

PRINCIPLE 7

Pain and Pleasure

Every leader has a thorn. Know yours.

The last six principles helped you to know how to define and achieve success from a godly perspective. I conclude this book with a word about the success we must all achieve within. One of the grave tragedies of our era is the lack of moral credibility among very public leaders. Our public square and pulpits are full of stories of the failures of rising stars.

Let me submit to you that public falls are often preceded by private stumbles. Whatever we finally see on the news or in social media results from previous battles lost to our weaknesses and struggles.

The scandals we see should be cautionary tales for all of us who want to lead well. They are not, however, opportunities for us to talk about how flawed they are. Rather, they are parables by which we understand the tragicomic reality of all human beings. We are at this moment not all that we should be. We don't like talking about sin much anymore, but I've lived long enough to know that sin is real. It's real in me, it's real in you, and it's real in the world. One of the Greek New Testament words for sin can be translated "missing the mark." In a very real sense, to sin is to miss the mark, to not be all we should be. Romans 3:23 tells us that all of us have sinned and fall short of the glory of God. When we seek our glory over God's, we have sinned.

Taking inventory in this way is sobering. Our present culture tells us that there's nothing wrong with us, that every wrong is "out there" somewhere. We are told not to take personal responsibility, but to always blame someone or something else for what we do wrong. To be sure, there are things that happen to us for which we are not to blame. There are indeed systems of oppression that hold us back. These truths don't conflict with the truth that there are things in us that make us do things that we wouldn't do otherwise. Paul puts it this way in Romans 7: 15-20

15 For I do not understand my own actions. For I do not do what I want, but I do the very thing I hate. 16 Now if I do what I do not want, I agree with the law, that it is good. 17 So now it is no longer I who do it, but sin that dwells within me. 18 For I know that nothing good dwells in me, that is, in my flesh.

For I have the desire to do what is right, but not the ability to carry it out. 19 For I do not do the good I want, but the evil I do not want is what I keep on doing. 20 Now if I do what I do not want, it is no longer I who do it, but sin that dwells within me.

We should not read this and think that we are just horrible people. No, we are created in the image of God and have wonderful gifts and potential from God. At the same time, there are things within us that set us back from God's best for our lives. When we fall short, we are not living up to all we can be and should be. As a Christ follower, I know that I am what I am by God's grace alone. Whatever success I've achieved has in a real way been in spite of me. Leaders must humbly accept this if we are to avoid failure.

A few years ago, I had the pleasure of preaching a revival on the Mississippi Gulf Coast. The pastor of the church is an older gentleman and I enjoyed the conversations we had about his life and ministry. Now in his

80's, he had much to share. One of the unforgettable lessons he offered me was one on integrity. I will always remember him saying, "Son, there's a difference between weakness and wickedness. We all have weaknesses, but we all don't have to be wicked." WOW! That floored me.

It is true that all of us have weaknesses. If you say you don't, then your weakness must be lying. Anyway, the point is if we understand our weaknesses, we can receive deliverance from the Lord, or at least know how to manage them. Otherwise, our weakness can get so twisted to the point that they become wickedness and ultimately lead to our downfall.

It is said that money magnifies what's in a person, so if they end up falling into temptation, it's because they were always prone to that thing. This saying suggests that not everyone is prone to fall, thus, money may only magnify the good in us if we don't have a weakness. I believe this saying is misguided.

All of us have something within us that can lead us astray. Money and access only give greater opportunity to do the things we couldn't do when we had limited resources. The truth is all of us have a weakness because all of us are sinners in need of grace. All of us are human, and to be human is to be frail.

Throughout my leadership journey, I've seen my share of pastors, politicians, and successful people fall from grace. Instead of pointing my finger at them, I've tried to understand them better. More often than not, they fell because their weakness got the best of them. Many of them wrestled with that thing for years. Maybe it was lust for sex or power. Maybe it was a craving for more money. For most leaders, our weakness is insecurity. At some point in our lives, we were made to feel insecure. We may have come to be insecure about our looks, our finances, our relationships, or our capacity to succeed. Because our society defines vulnerability as antithetical to leadership, we end up masking our pain with pleasures that make us forget that we are dust. Sometimes the sex addict is running away from the fear of not being wanted. Sometimes the embezzler is afraid of being poor again.

Whatever our weakness is, and however we got it, we must confront it honestly. You cannot change what you do not face. I encourage you to take seriously whatever weakness you have before it becomes your wickedness. What a shame it would be for us to be public successes and private failures all because we didn't take the time to search our souls and deal intentionally with our stuff.

Listen, we all have something. Adam and Eve wanted the one thing they didn't have despite everything they did have. Noah got drunk. Abraham lied. Jacob was a destiny stealer. Joseph was immature and arrogant with his dreams. Moses was a murderer and had a stuttering problem. Gideon was insecure about where he was from. Sampson had a lust problem. So did David and

Solomon. Jeremiah felt he was too young to preach. Hosea has marital issues. John the Baptist doubted. The disciples weren't reliable. Martha was anxious. Paul had a thorn.

And God used them anyway.

And he said unto me, My grace is sufficient for thee: for my strength is made perfect in weakness. Most gladly therefore will I rather glory in my infirmities, that the power of Christ may rest upon me.

2 Corinthians 12:9

ABOUT THE AUTHOR

With nearly two decades of leadership and ministry experience, CJ is an anointed voice for reform and transformation in the church and society. He is a family man, pastor, professor, theological thinker, and much sought after thought leader changing his generation, one community at a time. His ministry radiates from Jackson, Mississippi, where he pastors the historic Mt. Helm Baptist Church, and expands to reach people and places around the nation and world. A scholar and mentor, CJ also serves as Director of Student Religious Life at Alcorn State University. He has degrees from the University of Mississippi, Duke University Divinity

School, and Wesley Biblical Seminary. He and his wife, Allison, have twin sons.

www.ingramcontent.com/pod-product-compliance
Lightning Source LLC
Chambersburg PA
CBHW071332190426
43193CB00041B/1753